This writing book belongs to:

Before you start to write letters and words, warm up your pencil by tracing over the dotted lines on this page.

We're doing our warm up, too!

These 'warm-up activities' will help make your child more confident at using a pencil. You could write his name lightly on the line for him to trace over.

Follow the paths

The racing cars are lined up at the start. Trace the paths they take to get to the finish.

These simple tracing activities will help your child to develop better pencil control. Encourage him to make long flowing movements.

Finish the patterns to link the pictures of things that start with the same letter sound.

Say the names of the things with your child. Emphasise the sound the first letter makes. Can he think of other things starting with that sound? These patterns will help your child when he starts to join letters.

Letter patterns

These letters are all round.

Trace the letters.

car

c c c c c c c

a a a a a a a

ants

d d d d d d d

dog

Look at the picture and say the word.
Write the first letter sound you hear.

c at

d uck

a pple

Practising letters with similar patterns together will help your child to develop correct letter formation. The starting point for each letter is indicated by a dot.

Trace the letters.

queen

gate

orange

Look at the picture and say the word.
Write the first letter sound you hear.

octopus

queen

goat

Letter patterns

Start at the top and go down straight. Watch out for the curve at the bottom!

Trace the letters.

leaf

table

ill

Look at the picture and say the word.
Write the first letter sound you hear.

Lion

tent

invitation

*Left-handed children will find it easier to cross the **t** from right to left, the opposite to right-handers. Explain that we dot the **i** after writing the letter.*

Trace the letters.

up

u u u u u u

y y y y y y

yellow

Look at the picture and say the word.
Write the first letter sound you hear.

umbrella

yogurt

Letter patterns

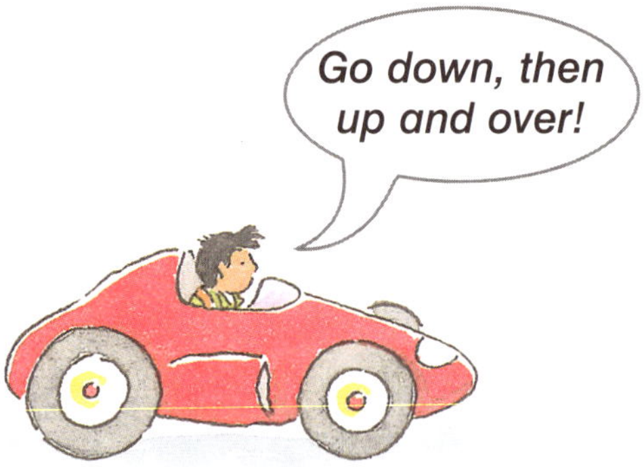
Go down, then up and over!

Trace the letters.

r r r r r

rabbit

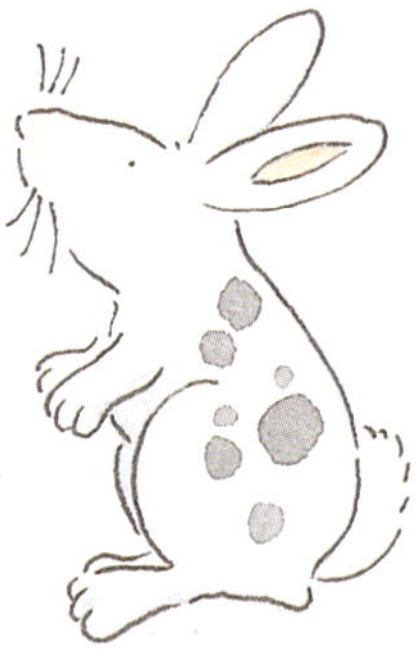

n n n n n

nose

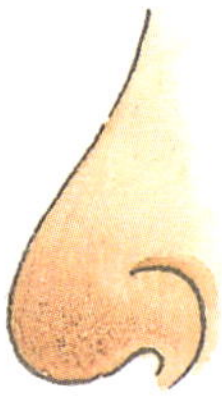

m m m m

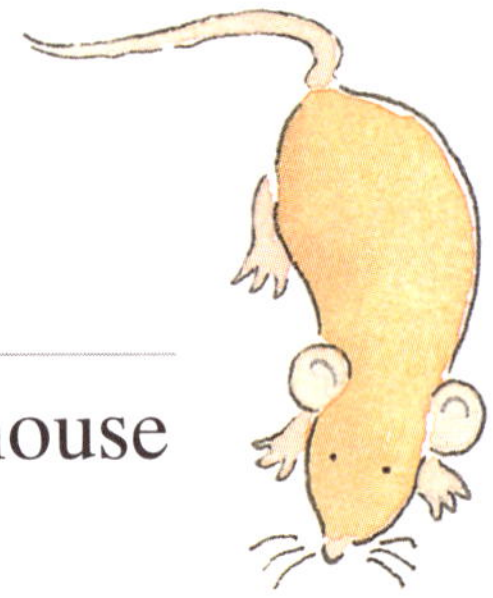

mouse

Look at the picture and say the word.
Write the first letter sound you hear.

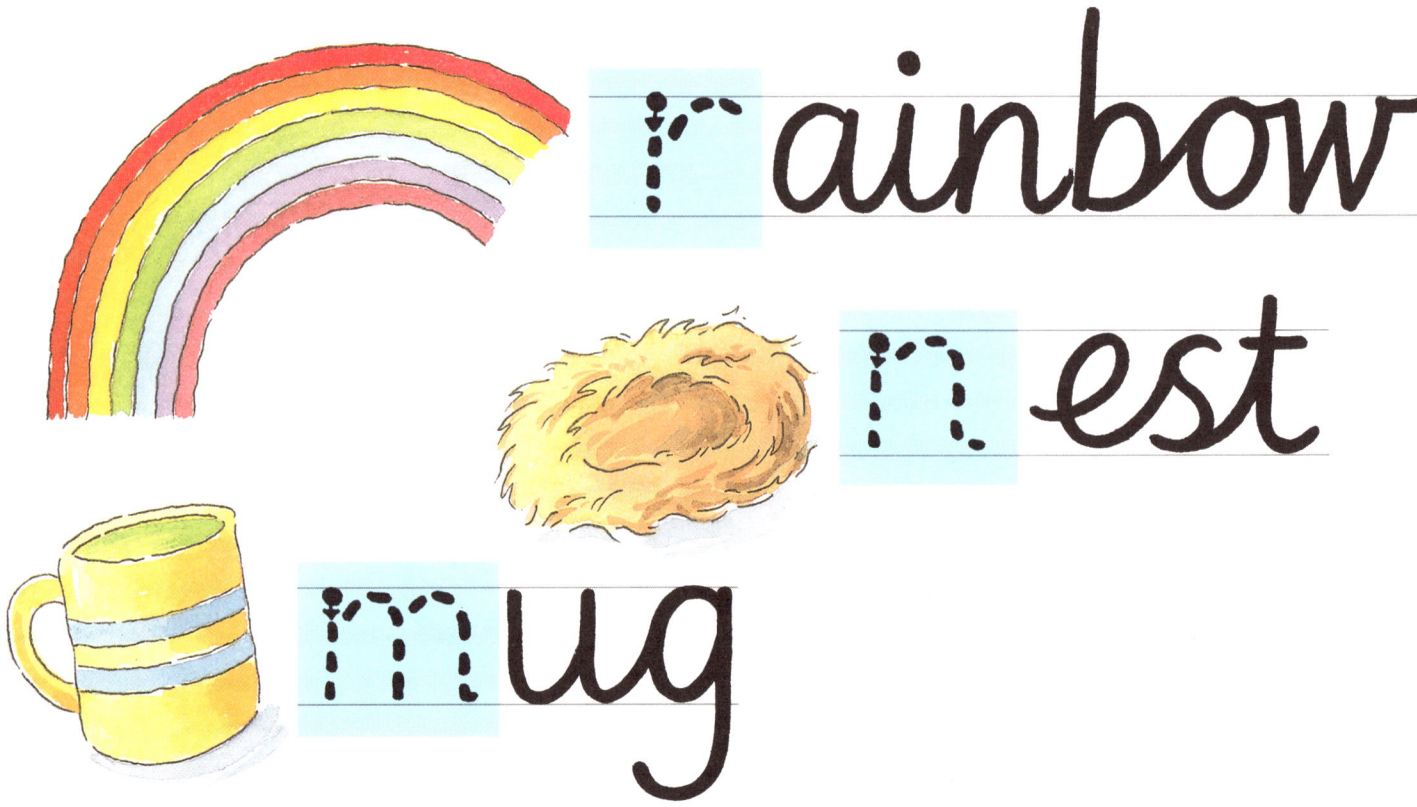

rainbow

nest

mug

Trace the letters.

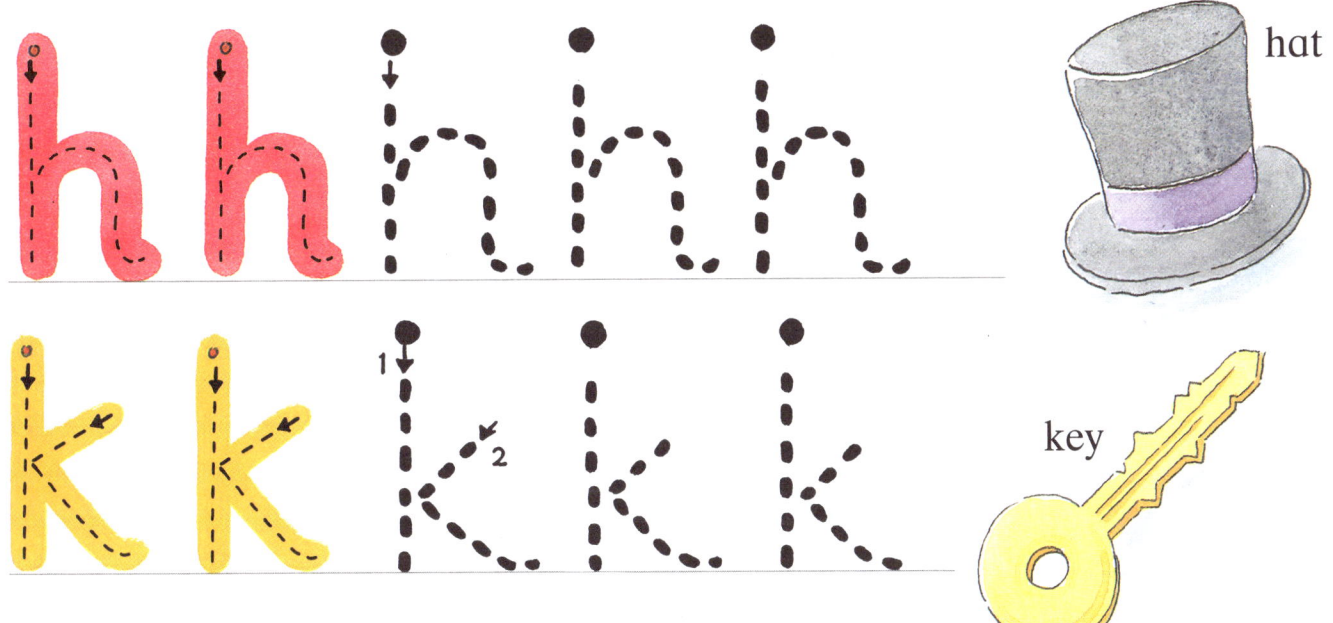

h h h h h

hat

k k k k k

key

Look at the picture and say the word.
Write the first letter sound you hear.

horse

kite

Your child will develop better handwriting if he sits comfortably at a table to write. Give him a cushion to sit on if the chair is too low. Ideally his feet should be flat on the floor.

Letter patterns

Here are more letters that go down, then up and over.

Trace the letters.

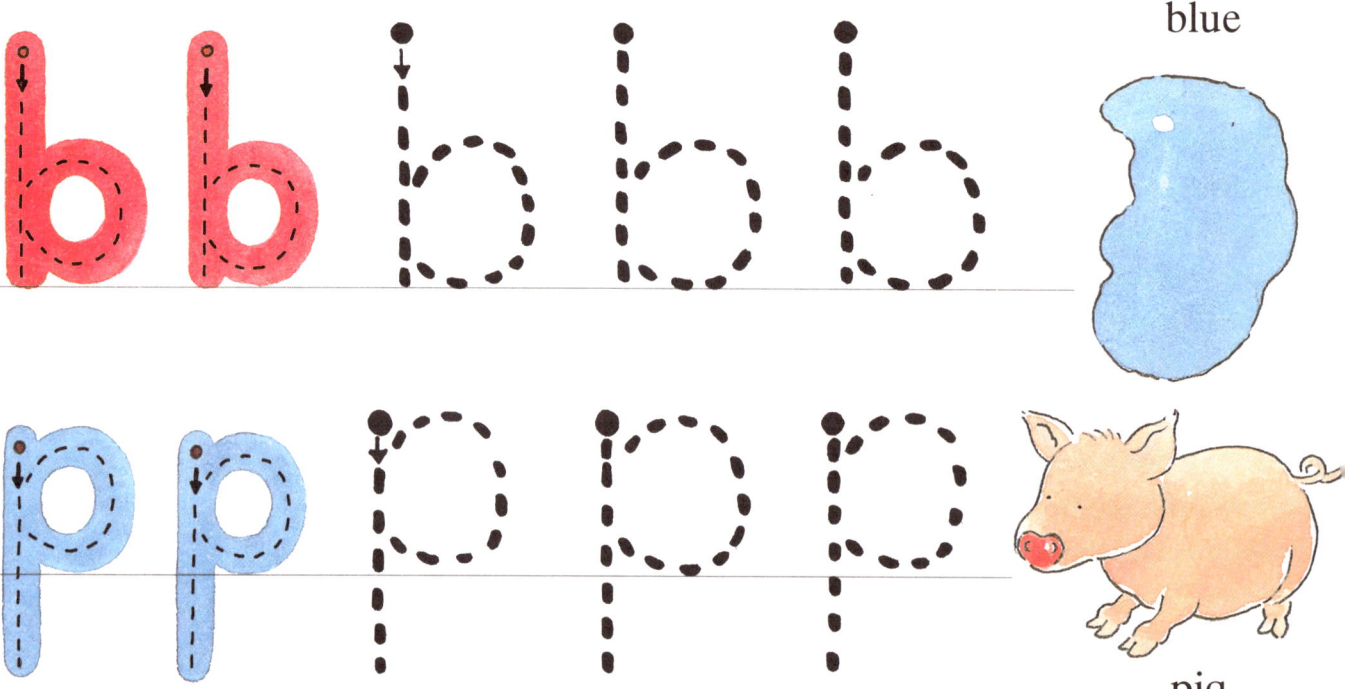

blue

pig

Look at the picture and say the word.
Write the first letter sound you hear.

b ed

p ie

Take care going round the bends!

Trace the letters.

e e e e e

egg

s s s s s

sun

Look at the picture and say the word.
Write the first letter sound you hear.

elephant

sandwich

Make sure your child is holding the paper steady with the hand that is not writing.

Letter patterns

Trace the letters.

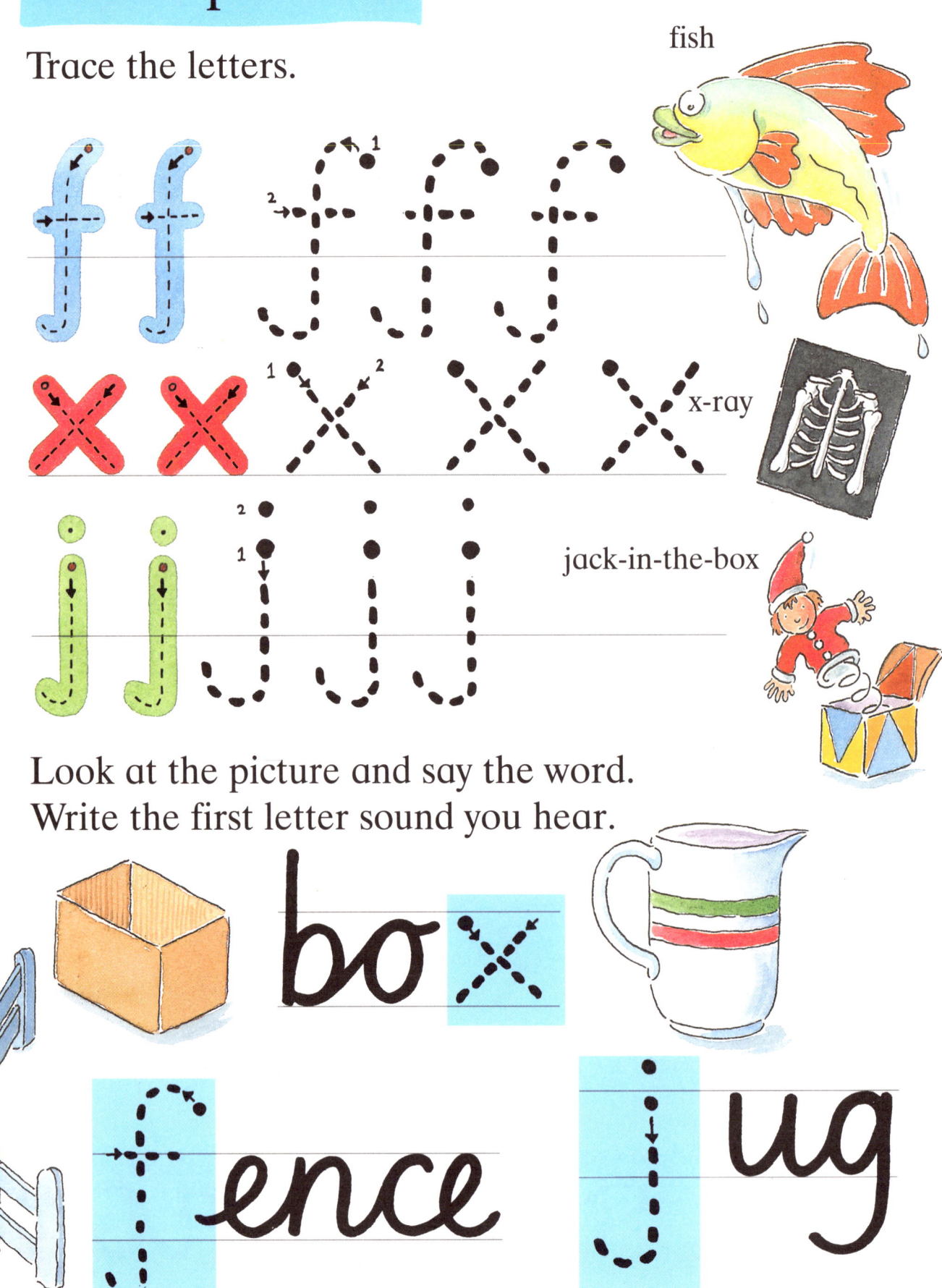

fish

x-ray

jack-in-the-box

Look at the picture and say the word.
Write the first letter sound you hear.

bo x

f ence

j ug

*If your child is left-handed, show him how to cross the **f** from right to left.*
*Explain that we dot the **j** after writing the letter.*

Can you keep to the lines on these joined-up writing trails? When you have finished, wipe the page clean and have another go.

Copy writing

Choose what you'd like on your shopping list.
Ask an adult to write the word and then you copy it.
Wipe clean and make up another list.

apple

jam

milk

pear

ice cream

cake

Making and sending cards is lots of fun. What does this card say? Practise copying the writing underneath the words. Then wipe clean and write again.

Come to

my party

Make a pattern around the edge of your card.

Who would you like to write to? Ask a grown-up to write their name and address here.

Now *you* copy it on to the envelope below and draw a stamp.

Simplify the address by just using the street name, eg 'Mary Brown, 5 Spring Street'.

Trace the letters.

Watch out for the sharp corners!

v v v v v v v v
van 

w w w w w w
watch

z z z z z z
zebra 

Look at the picture and say the word.
Write the first letter sound you hear.

Vase

Zip

Window

Letter patterns

Here are all the letters again. This is the order they appear in the alphabet. Trace the letters then practise writing them here.

Look for the starting point on each letter and follow the arrows.

*The four line guide will help your child to make all the letters a similar size. Point out how most letters sit on the same line. A few, such as **b** and **d**, stick up, whilst others such as **j** and **p**, go down.*

m m   n n   o o

p p   q q   r r

s s   t t   u u

v v   w w   x x

y y   z z

Capital letters

Let's go to the capitals!

Trace and copy the letters here.

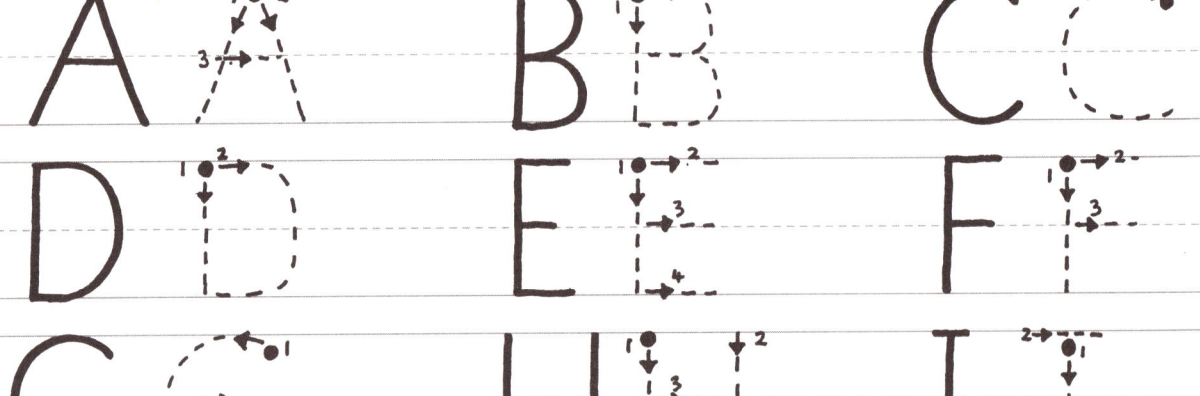

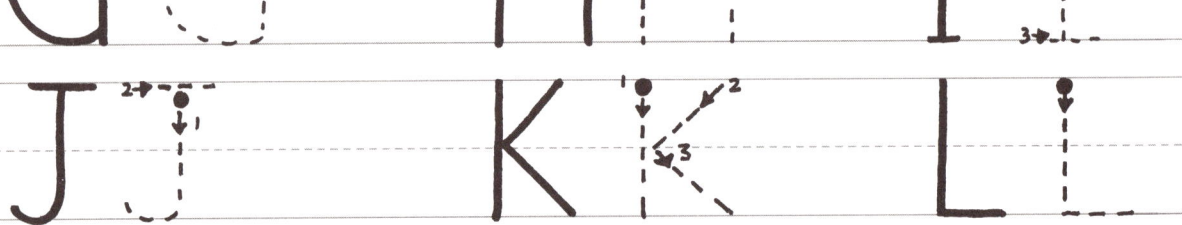

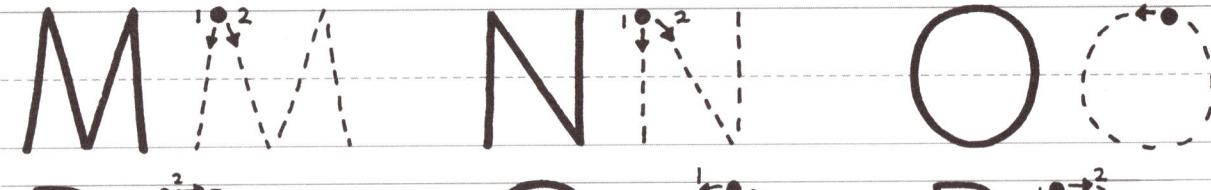

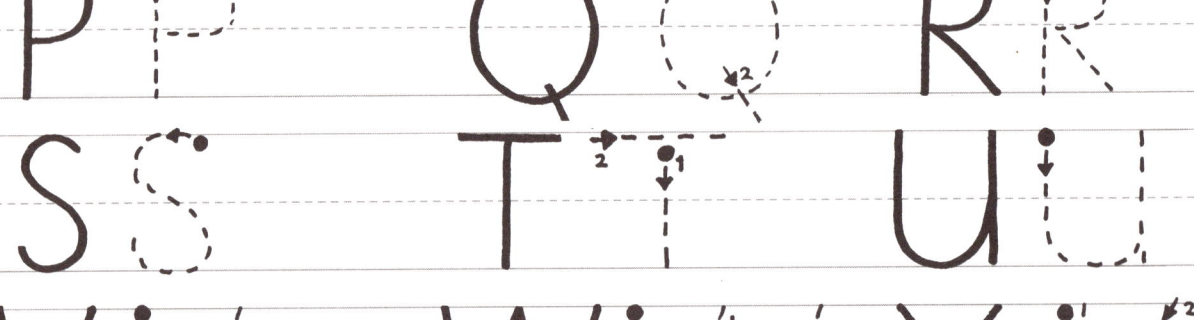

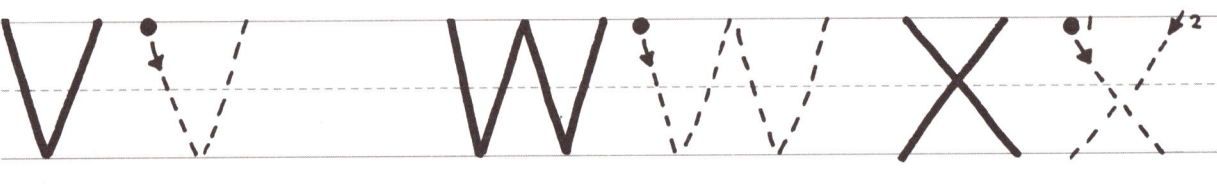

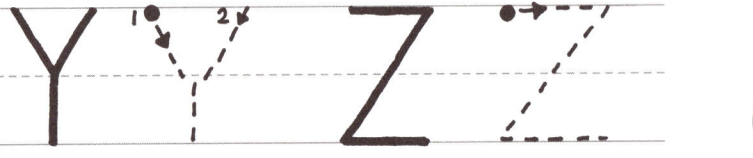

Well done! You've worked hard!

When you write names, only the first letter of each word has a capital letter. Write the capital letters to finish these names.

Sammy Snake

Penny Panda

Ask someone to write your name here.

Now *you* copy your name here.

Write your child's name carefully for him to copy. You could add some starting dots to remind him where to begin.

Joined-up letters

The letters are all joined-up for the animal parade.
Trace over the letter patterns as the animals go by.

Aim for enthusiasm and staying power, rather than accuracy at this stage.

Trace over the letter patterns as the animals go by.

a a a a

d d d d

m m m m

o o o o

Words with 'at'

Practise writing these joined-up words.

cat

hat

rat

mat

While the lazy cat sat on a mat
the daring rat climbed over the hat.

*Encourage your child to hold the pencil in a relaxed way between the thumb and
forefinger supported by the middle finger.*

Words with 'in'

Practise writing these joined-up words.

bin

pin

tin

fin

The fish wiggled his fin and said 'What a din!'
as the tin filled with pins fell into the bin.

Words with 'an'

Practise writing these joined-up words.

man  van

pan  hand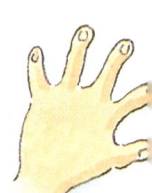

The delivery man opened his van and gave Jan a hand with her new pots and pans.

Words with 'ee'

Practise writing these joined-up words.

bee  tree

three **3** knee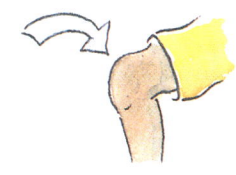

As Jean sat in the tree,
three bees sat on her knee.

Point out to your child how these words all end with the same letters and sound.
Explain that when words end with the same sound we say that they rhyme.

Words with 'oo'

Tip: cross the **t** in stool after you've finished writing the word.

Practise writing these joined-up words.

pool    *stool*

goose    *foot*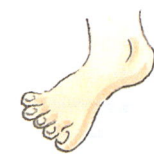

As Tom sat with one foot in the pool, his goose jumped up and down on the stool.